I love that you're my

Dad

because

I Love You Because Books
www.riverbreezepress.com

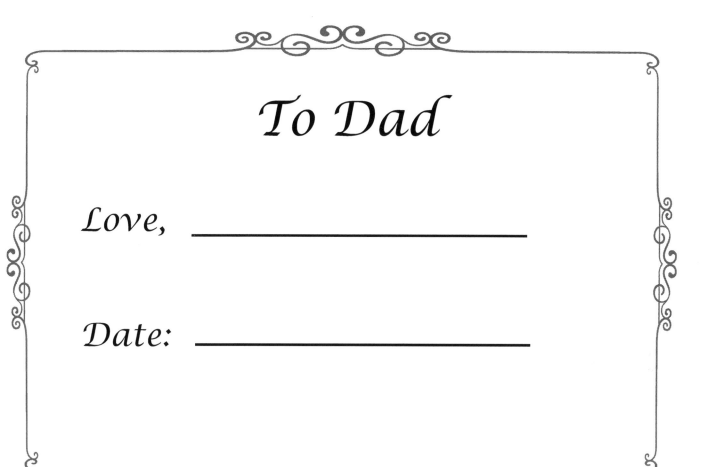

To Dad

Love, _____

Date: _____

The best thing about you is your

_____

Thank you for being patient with me when

_____

You are better than a

_____

You should win the grand prize for

_____

You make me feel special when

_____

Dad, I love you more than

_____

I love when you tell me about

_____

I love when we

_____

together

You taught me how to

_____

I know you love me because

_____

I wish I could

---

*as well as
you do*

Dad, I love that we have the same

_____

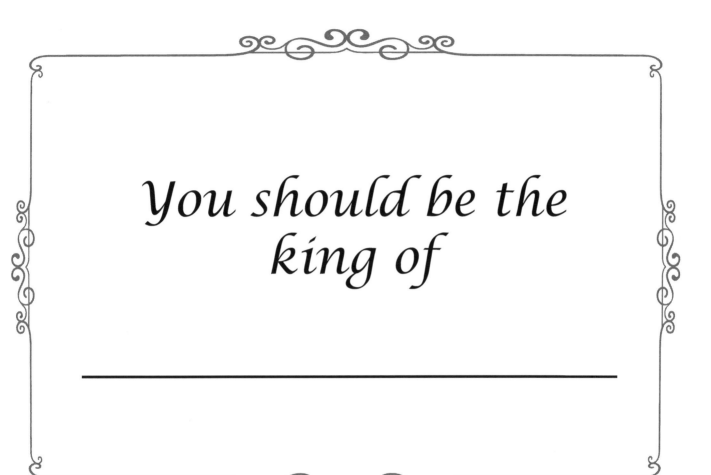

You should be the
king of

_____

You have an amazing talent for

_____

Dad, you make me laugh when you

_____

I wish I had more time to

_____

with you

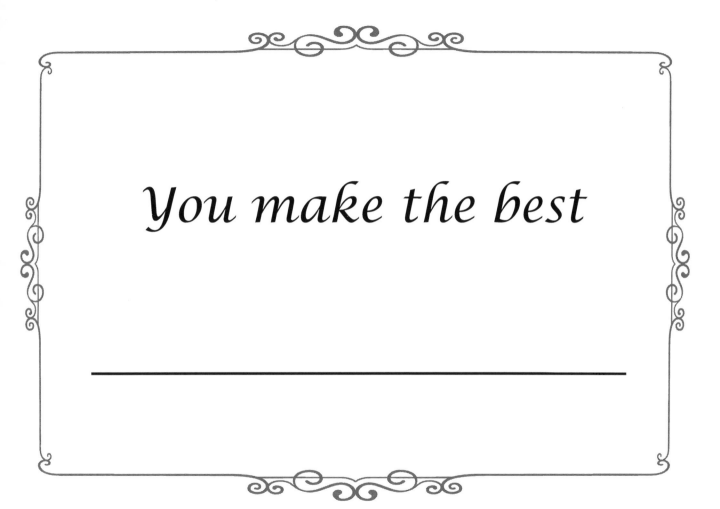

You make the best

_____

You have
inspired me to

_____

If I could give you anything it would be

I would love to go

_____

with you

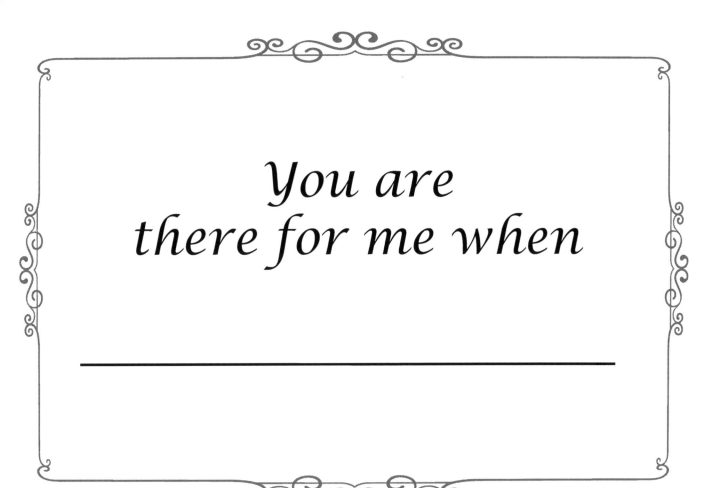

You are
there for me when

_____

Dad, I love you because you are

_____

Made in the USA
Monee, IL
13 December 2020

52841109R00028